BRISTOL RIOTS

" RT @Lucy_Art: Banksy produces petrol bomb 'art' to help anti-Tesco campaigners in Stokes Croft, Bristol http://t.co/tVQV7y4 "

billphilpot

May 4, 2011 at 16:27

Bristol Riots is a photographic collection of the original demonstrations against the siting of a Tesco store on the main Cheltenham Road into Stokes Croft and the riot in the Spring of 2011 which took place after police raided a squatted building opposite the Tesco store.

Riot police moved in with horses and dogs in the early evening and the ensuing riot spread from Stokes Croft into St Pauls and Montpelier. The police eventually retreated in the early hours and the rioters trashed the new Tesco shop.

Where the national media failed to report the event that night, the news of the riot quickly spread via social networks, providing an up to date view into the riot and its effects on the area of Stokes Croft. This digital journalism sits along side the elegant photography of the event allowing for an insight into the unfolding of the riot.

The riot is the dialectic between squat and supermarket, standing opposite each other lie two extremes of socio-spatiality architecture; and at the centre is the riot...

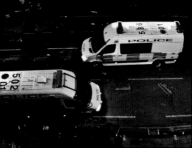

©Jonathon Taphouse

©Kai Heron

©Kai Heron

©Kai Heron

©Matt Redmond

©Matt Redmond

©Mike Taylor

©Andy Webb

©Matt Redmond

©Kai Heron

www.flickr.com/photos/kaiagainstkai/
©Kai Heron

©Kai Heron

©Andy Webb

©Matt Redmond

©Jonathon Taphouse

©Ross Harrison

©Kai Heron

©Andy Webb

©Andy Webb

©Marc Jay

©Matt Redmond

©Matt Redmond

©Andy Webb

©Matt Redmond

©Kai Heron

©Andy Webb

©Matt Redmond

©Matt Redmond
www.flickr.com/photos/stringberd/

©Ross Harrison

©Jonathon Taphouse

©Jonathon Taphouse

©Jonathon Taphouse

13

>

> I return to Bristol from the wedding I've been photographing all day, only to find police blocking Cheltenham Road, 7 Riot vans at the ready. Last time I saw this, it was the police / bailiffs removing squatters from the TESCO site, so i knew it was going be something BIG... I pulled up on some double yellows and grabbed my camera.

> On talking to the police, no-one could tell me what was going on. They just said that they didn't know, but suggested at an eviction from the squat opposite (if they told us the truth, maybe none of this would have escalated?). Locals evacuating the sectioned off area were talking about possible petrol bombs.

> A line of welsh police armoured with helmets, shields and batons were stopping people entering the area. It was peaceful, but people were confused as to what was going on. Suddenly there was music, and a small group wearing black bandannas over their faces marched up to the police, trailer with massive stereo in tow. One individual aggressively squared up to the guards, and was immediately thrown back by one of the officers with a double-handed shove to the chest. In hindsight, this was the moment things went wrong...

Jonathon Taphouse   pro

http://www.flickr.com/photos/jonathantaphouse/5653010825/

RT @Karlwareham: "Police seized items described at "potential petrol bombs" in #stokescroft . Protestors have gone way too far." Potential petrol bomb=bottle "

bruuns
April 22, 2011 at 9:32

> Squat on #stokescroft is being evicted. 'Copter above us for half an hour. 10+ riot vans.Road closed http://twitpic. com/4nqawe "

pearcafe

April 21, 2011 at 22:12

> " So if the squatters near Stokes Croft had petrol bombs, the police had to raid it. Am I wrong? Is it ok to petrol bomb a supermarket? "
>
> jamgyal
> April 22, 2011 at 11:10

> " Police quote re arrests in Stokes Croft: "a very real threat to the local community". Couldn't sum up the affect of Tesco better. "
>
> onlyabeggar
> April 22, 2011 at 11:41

“ @Shep_Shep_Shep #stokescroft was about both the
Tesco and the squatters. It was community defence and
solidarity. ”

Sophia CR
April 22, 2011 at 10:05

please All
and our right to non-explosive shopping!
us our rig
Peaceful
Oligarc

Quick someone declare #stokescroft a royal wedding street
party and David Cameron will tell the cops to stop their red
tape & interfering ''

TenPercent
April 22, 2011 at 1:13

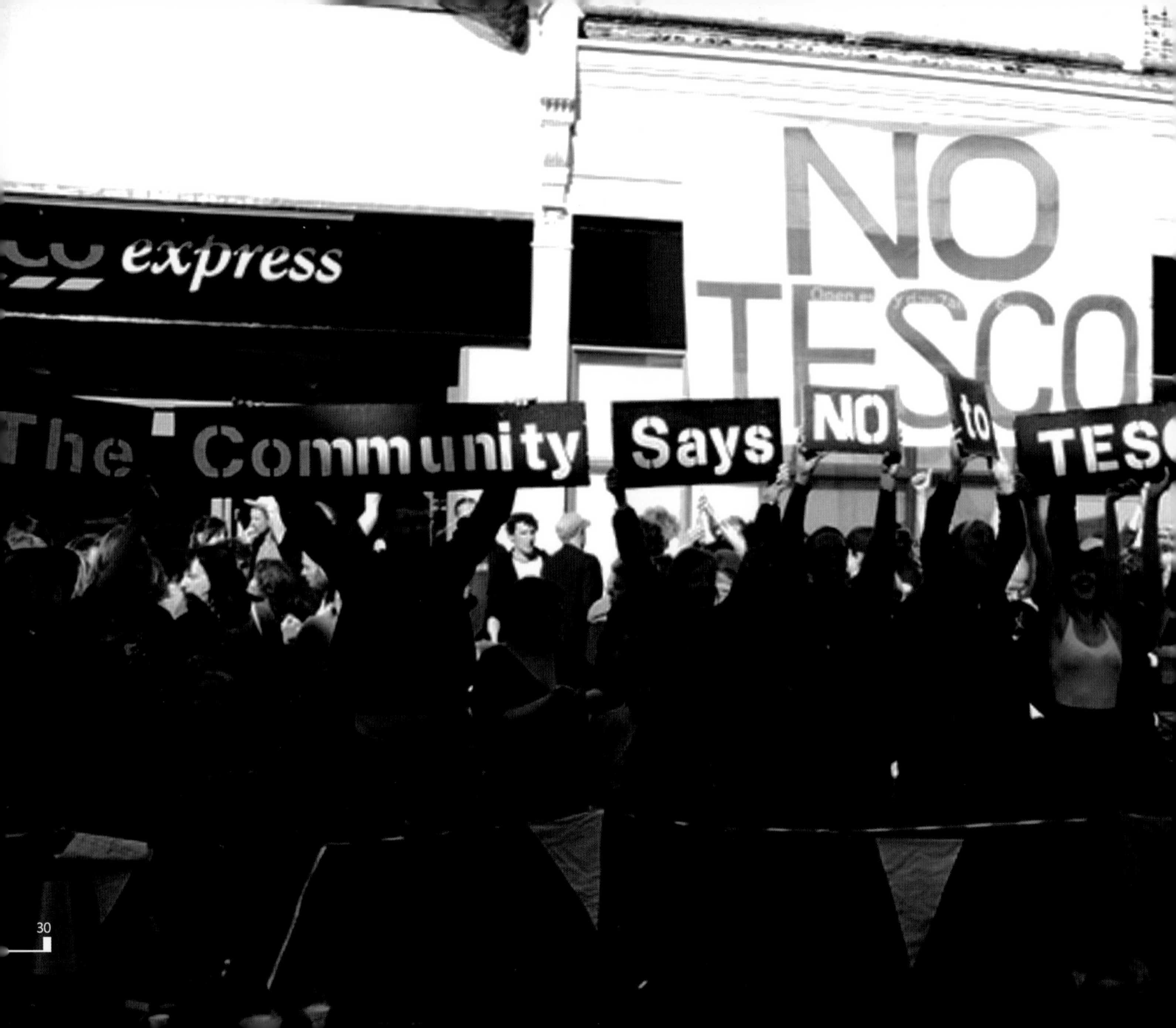
express
NO
TESCO
The Community Says NO to TES

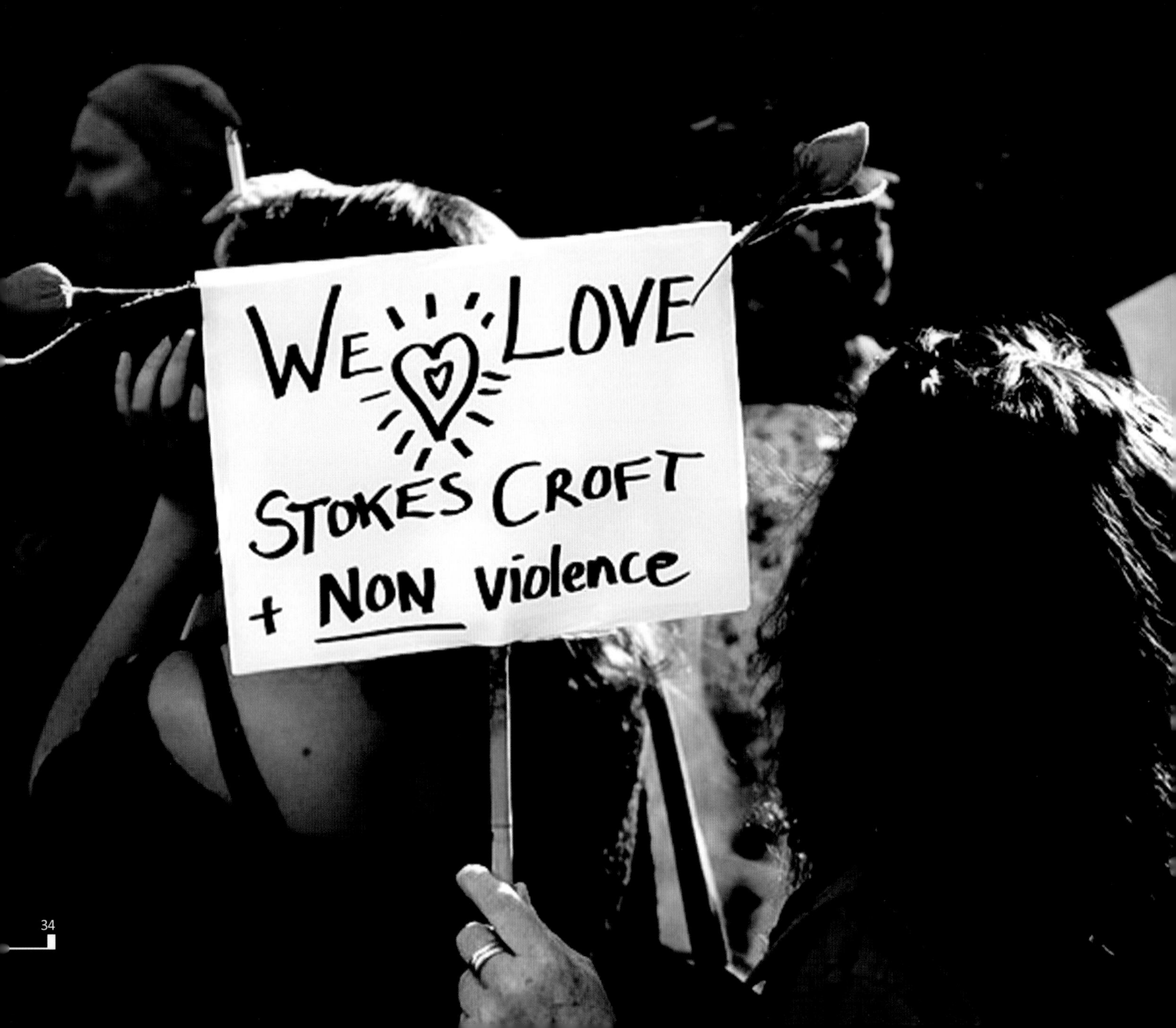
WE LOVE
STOKES CROFT
+ NON violence

“ I mean punching a police horse over a Tesco, don't lose respect #stokescroft #increasethepeace ”

Kergozou
 April 22, 2011 at 10:10

> Woke to tweets and news reports of rioting on #stokescroft in Bristol. What's the trigger - squatter eviction or unwanted Tesco? "

Amy_Potter
April 22, 2011 at 10:07

39

Local Banksy graffiti

66 Just saw a video of Tesco in stokes croft getting smashed up. People are pathetic. 99

cold_blue87
April 22, 2011 at 11:30

66 Appears it was Stokes Croft the Police helicopter was watching last night... Should have gone down there for a BBQ. Tesco was on fire! 99

paulsheward
April 22, 2011 at 11:30

66 I'm glad that Tesco in Stokes Croft got smashed up,I was bored of all the peaceful stuff, people finally stood up,did what they shoulda done 99

AlexStedman
April 22, 2011 at 11:42

CAFE ▪ BAR ▪ GALLERY ▪ CINEMA

the **Arts** hou

POLICE

" All BBC can say is 4 police officers hurt? No mention of
Tesco's or police brutality? http://bbc.in/gLt7V5 #stokescroft "

SirioCD
April 22, 2011 at 9:45

" #Stokescroft Friend hit across face with riot shield and
struck with baton 1 metre from home. Ear stitched. Bad po. "

20thCFlicks
April 22, 2011 at 10:13

>

> A couple of times the police shouted 'charge!' and then rushed us- people turned and fled or were trampled. Each time they advanced people tried to ask them why they were doing this. An officer I spoke to said that they didn't have time to work out who was a threat and who wasn't, and they were trying to prevent violence. Then a member of the line shouted 'advance!' and he started shoving me down the road with his riot shield. As the line came down the road there was a feeling of panic in the air. The police tactics made no sense- why were they forcing us further and further down the street? Where did they want us to end up? Hundreds of people poured down from the rest of the Montpelier area and neighbouring St Pauls.

BristolFloozie
@BristolFloozie Bristol

http://www.counterfire.org/ index.php/articles/163- resisting-austerity/12066-the-battle-of-stokes-croft-an- account-of-the-riot

"As far as I can tell there's a group of #stokescroft protesters coming my way again. Plenty of people are joining now from both directions."

rossoh
April 22, 2011 at 1:36

" Walked nearly 4 miles getting to a bed last night! Avoiding the
Stokes Croft riot. "

ImCask
April 22, 2011 at 11:43

" So trashing property and other
best way to get your message

84

“ Mr Cloggins & I are hugely unimpressed with the "Stokes Croft Riots" in Bristol last night. Just so you know. ”

Cloggins
April 22, 2011 at 11:43

“ Well I'll be using my local Tesco on Stokes Croft as much as possible now. Crusty tossers. ”

Rockerq
April 22, 2011 at 12:03

Riot-truth is to epistemology what shoplifting is to capitalism…

[assemblage] This text, these words operate as riot–prose (part–science, part riot–fiction) a mimesis of the anarchic structure, organization, apparatus and transitions of the riot re–territorialized qua theoretico–ideological event. Examining six autonomous riot thematics: the riot as dialectic; the space, body and intelligence systems of the police, riot territorialization; riots as mediated events – discourse, actions, protests as modes of signification; power/knowledge relationships; and finally the aftermath – police methods for interrogation and (re)presentation of the riot. Riot is translated imperfectly as partial, rhizomatic[1], fluxive, impure and contingent, multiple and unofficial; preserving the localities and specificity of the riot–text as agent provocateur.

[dialecticism] The riot is the dialectic between squat and supermarket. The synthesis of: consumerism and its antithesis: the squat. Standing opposite each other lie two extremes of socio–spatiality architecture; at the centre is the riot. Framed by a quasi–legal squat – fractured identities of anarchy/bedlam; programmeless schisms disavowing time-space functionalism. Lying opposite is Tesco©; space of late capitalism and post–modern superstructure – the globalized chain of stores selling commodities organized with brutal efficiency; a production system of delivery processes, supply chain mechanisms and Fordist labour relations: commodified, privatized, fetishized[2].

[cyber>body-space] The riot–police are a cyborg discontinuity. Police–space is institutionalised, operationalized and disciplined through powerful mechanisms operating on/through it. The police–body is controlled, constructed, architecturalized through the deployment of hypertrophied anti–protestor grafts/implants: helmets, face–masks, body armour, shin–pads, visors – all of which are extended by an infrastructure of terror: batons, tear–gas masks, dogs, whips, tazers. Technological police–space is the most rapidly developing, with the deployment of machines, software and media employed to effect power. Police–bodies have been tagged and digitally coded to connect into an (anti)body. The police riot–body forms a larger structure, organised mechanistically in grid/row/column with control units relaying radio messages back and forth. Each of these mobile grids of defence are then augmented by cyborg technology; the data–tagged police (no longer endowed with names, but abstracted numbers and codes) send and receive messages real–time to the police helicopter, which controls three dimensional sky–space. This data-scape is simultaneously connected to CCTV cameras and their team of video–controllers, who manipulate real–time the mobile police–architectures through space. Police–bodies become a hybrid of machine–technology, information systems, political will and autonomous external intelligence[3]. The location of control is dissipated across/through the body on the ground, to the ranks of bodies formed by the police, to the (remote) controllers at the HQ to the helicopter circling above.

1.   Deleuze, G. and Guattari, F. (1988). Thousand Plateaus: Capitalism and Schizophrenia. London: Athlone Press.
2.   Lefebvre, H. (1991) The Production of Space. Oxford: Blackwell.
3.   Haraway, D. (1991) Simians, Cyborgs and Women: The Reinvention of Nature. New York: Routledge.

[cyber>body–space] Each point of intelligence(s) sends contradictory enmeshed signals, dissonant orders, tropes and exteroceptive strategies... the body in space behaves as a differential field... the 'riotbody' is multiple: a riot–body$_X$ (the assembled collectif) the riot body$_Y$ (the individualized entities) the body–riot$_Z$ (body as tool>weapon>point of target>dispositif[4]). Who is in control? No longer relevant as a question; due to the hybridity of the policing organization. The question–politic remains What is in control? The specification procedures for controlling a riot, practice manuals, guidance and training methods produce an auto–response knowledge; the control of the individual body evanesces with corporate responses and control mechanisms, and orders from higher authorities. The police–body momentarily manifests as frighteningly inert, yet ethically combustible. The technology–organism–police–state–individual as a blurred archipelago/assemblage[5] has reconceptualized as a transformative ideological space that has developed ultra vires.

[territorialization] Riots are power–relation conglomerates; not just through force, but articulated thorough the problematic narrative of auto–riot apparatus and accession of intelligence(s). Protests maintain, constitute and generate multiple power ethnologies post hoc. Auto–riotic systems of power assemble a correlative constitution in the terrestrial field of protest and unofficial knowledge. Power resides in space; each city block generating its own political morphology. The question of power embedded in the urban fabric is not new, the spatio–problematic was evident during the riots of the French Revolution. The rioters against the Ancien Regime could not maintain power from the embryonic riot–spaces; instead, once the revolutionaries began the operations required for control of the State, they were forced to occupy the spaces of the State. Sustained riots must go beyond its embryonic territory of relations; and re–territorialize those parts of the city where power emanates. The Arab Spring exemplifies the necessity to shift the act of rioting from liminal spaces to centred spaces, as in Tahrir Square in Egypt, Pearl Roundabout in Bahrain and Tunisia, Algeria, Libya... re–territorialization of the riot is linked to the alter-articulation and maintenance of power.

4.   Foucault, M. (1977) "The Confession of the Flesh". In: Power/ Knowledge Selected Interviews and Other Writings. London: Harvester.
5.   Landa, M. D. (2006) A New Philosophy of Society: Assemblage Theory and Social Complexity. London: Continuum.

[mediator] Riot is a festival; a carnival of violence and immane protest, of railing against the norms of action; it enables and produces intersubjective taboos, exiled utterances and intrastitial signification[6]. The political co–ordinates of the carnival–riot disseminate a practice of unattenuated transgressions. The riot is paradoxical, it is both destructive and self–destructive; it has the capacity to detonate the socio–political power/knowledge apparatus. The process of dialogism disavows the formal/official knowledge base; signification voids the regimes of governmentality. Riot trans–disciplinarity invades the liminal and displaces without requirement for authentication but seeks its own conditions of emergence. It intervenes at extra–territorial boundaries… rarified and fluxive "always interpretative, critical and partial"[7]. The profane and grotesque of the riot–carnival are mediated through membership of crowd as social relations – the crowd are the riot, there are no spectators – no spectacle[8] amidst the suspension of hierarchic distinctions where riots peel back the immutability of formal knowledge/practice and seed alternatives[9]. Local skirmishes flourish as infractions in global generalities; rarely ambivalent but imperfect, disjunctive temporalities.

[power/knowledge] Etymologically, riot(e) comes from ancient French, meaning 'to debate'. Thus riots have a discursive quality: expressed multiply[10] through action, performative utterances, placards, and enunciatory modalities as part of a semiotic dispositif. Petrol bombs, peace poetry, civil disobedience, immolation, aerosols, desecration, aburdism, raasta roko, inciting agencies and non–conformism merge as an imbroglio of politico–performative resistance[11]. Ontologically, the multiple diaspora of the protestors defy the normative genealogy of a hegemonic monologue; resisting the homogeneity and obliterative totalitarianism of the grand narrative[12]. An ephemeral riot ontology erupts into existence briefly and violently before leaving striated traces on reality before dissipating into the void. In this moment of enunciative evacuation, partial decipherment of this apparatus criticus is operationalized. This non–correspondence… a futile liminality transgresses circumstances for an emergent genealogy of protest. The stated and unstateable possibilities of heterogenous localities fold, negotiate or collaborate through auto–destruct performance(s) creating ruptures, voids, extirpations in the narratives of the riot.

6.   Bakhtin, M. (1984) Discourse in the Novel. In: M. Holquist, ed. The Dialogic Imagination: Four Essays. Texas: Univ of Texas Press.
7.   Haraway, D. (1991:195) Simians, Cyborgs and Women: The Reinvention of Nature. New York: Routledge.
8.   Debord, G. (1970) Society of the Spectacle. Detroit: Black & Red.
9.   Bhabha, H. (1994) The Location of Culture. Oxon: Routledge.

10. Mol, A. (1999:75) Ontological Politics. A Word and Some Questions. In: Law, J. and Hasard, J. eds. Actor Network Theory and After. Oxford: Blackwell Publishers.
11. Latour, B. (1987) Science in Action. Cambridge, Mass.: Harvard Univ. Press.
12. Foucault, M. (2009) Madness and Civilization. New York: Routledge.

[post–hoc] The post–riot (re)presentation of the rioters by the Police Authority is through CCTV shots of the most wanted suspects laid out in a grid as digitized panoptican. This procedure unlocates specificity… decapitates individuals; decentres, deterritorializes, freeze–frames as body–less cadavre exquis. Framed in the white matrix of totalitarian space; an impersonal supergrid… the individual removed from the chaotic entangled context of the performative, messy, rampage–ism and absorbed into a dominatory and objectified (re)presentation. The riot's space is reconstituted, appropriated and detourned through spheres of mediated ideology into ennunciatory riot–space from local to generic; specificity lost to abstraction. Disassembly of the riot agglomeration into isolated entities; produced a temporo–foamic[13] structure of dissent. The supergrid enacts the language of science, accusatory, scientific, deterministic… this is a process of mistranslation perhaps, from the moment into the timeless, from action into ideology. Post–hoc surveillance attempts a dis–interpretation of events to colonize it's political utility, incarcerating in a rigid supergrid of juridical mechanisms and mediated, policed, carceral apparatus. But this quasi–sovereign dispositif is illegitimate; it misrepresents and dehumanizes simultaneous to an authoritarian monologue of conspiratorial facticity. The police as regulatory governmental (ir)rationality is ultimately revealed as a bastard of enforced synthetic consolidation.

13. Sloterdijk, P. (2004) Spharen III: Schaume. Frankfurt am Main: Suhrkamp.

CITY OF BRISTOL

BRISTOL
RIOTS
APRIL
2011